DARTMOUTH

A shortish guide

Robert Hesketh

Bossiney Books

Books about Dartmouth

Books on local subjects are well covered at the Tourist Information Centre, Dartmouth Library and the Dartmouth Community Bookshop

Allen, J S, *Thomas Newcomen Engineer 1663/4-1729* (Newcomen Society pamphlet, 1989)

Collinson, Don, *The Chronicles of Dartmouth, An Historical Yearly Log 1854-1954* (Richard Webb, Dartmouth, 2000). Excellent period photographs.

Davison, Brian K, *Dartmouth Castle* (English Heritage, 2000). Available at Dartmouth Castle.

Harrold, Jane and Porter, Richard, *Britannia Royal Naval College 1905-2005* (Richard Webb, Dartmouth, 2005)

Freeman, Ray, *Dartmouth and its Neighbours* (1990, reissued by Richard Webb, Dartmouth, 2009). Comprehensive history.

Freeman, Ray, *John Flavel: A Famous Dartmouth Puritan.* One of some 17 excellent pamphlets published by Dartmouth History Research Group.

Jaine, Tom, *Dartmouth: A Brief Historical Guide* (Dartmouth and Kingswear Society)

Risdon, John, *The River Dart* (Halsgrove, 2004)

White, Paul, *Shortish Walks – Torbay and Dartmouth* (Bossiney, 2006)

Websites

Good starting points are:

The Dartmouth Directory, www.dartmouth.org.uk/directory

Tourist Information Centre, www.discoverdartmouth.com (Tel 01803 834224)

Second edition 2012
First published 2007 by Bossiney Books Ltd
33 Queens Drive, Ilkley, LS29 9QW
www.bossineybooks.com
ISBN 978-1-906474-41-6

Acknowledgements
The maps on pages 9, 12, 19 and 32 are by Graham Hallowell.
All photographs are by the author except the following which are from the publishers' own collection: 5b and 28.
Printed in Great Britain by R Booth Ltd, Penryn, Cornwall

The brass in St Saviour's Church, in memory of John Hawley, c1342-1408, Dartmouth's leading merchant and privateer, who constructed the first Dartmouth castle

Dartmouth's history

A thousand years ago there was no Dartmouth. The low lying areas of what became the town were all underwater at high tide. The site was also dangerously exposed to seaborne Viking raids. As a result, the Saxon English ignored it and settled at Townstal on the hill above the Dart, hidden from the view of seafarers.

In the Domesday Book of 1086, Dartmouth was not mentioned (the name only became general in the 13th century) but Townstal was valued at ten shillings. It paid tax on half a hide and had two plough teams and two slaves. The five villagers and four smallholders had six cattle, forty sheep and fifteen goats between them. Clearly, it was an estate of low value, even by the standards of the time, its steep slopes mainly used for rough grazing.

With its deep water and shelter, the mouth of the Dart is a superb natural harbour, conveniently close to the Channel Islands, Normandy and Brittany. The conquering Normans appreciated this. They built houses and port facilities on higher ground to the north (Hardness) and to the south (Clifton) of the large creek which occupied the area that later became the centre of Dartmouth.

Development moved apace. In 1147 an international force of 164 ships assembled at Dartmouth and set sail for the Second Crusade.

Thirty-seven ships left the Dart to join the Third Crusade in 1190. Dartmouth played an important role in England's wars from then on, not least in the Hundred Years War, when it sent 31 vessels to the Great Blockade of Calais in 1346. Its greatest contribution was for D-Day, 1944, when 485 ships sailed from Dartmouth to Normandy, taking a whole day to clear the port.

When Henry II gained Bordeaux by marriage, Dartmouth began a lucrative wine trade that ensured its prosperity for 300 years. Wool, wheat and fish were its main exports, carried in sturdy little ships called cogs. Averaging 140 tons, cogs bore one large, square sail and were well able to defend themselves on the lawless seas. They earned their place on the town's arms.

Now an international port, Dartmouth gained its weekly market in 1231 and became a Royal Borough in 1327. Rough enterprise and war with France were the abiding themes of medieval Dartmouth, as shown in the life of John Hawley (*c* 1342-1408). Fourteen times mayor and twice MP, Hawley was both a leading merchant and a privateer.

England relied for its defence largely on armed merchant ships, licensed by the king as privateers. Hawley was among the shipmen from Dartmouth and Portsmouth who destroyed a French fleet in 1383, slaying all but nine men. They later captured 1500 casks of French wine and sailed up the river Seine, destroying four ships and capturing four more. Back on shore, Mayor Hawley was ordered to build Dartmouth's first castle in 1388.

Avoiding this castle, an invading Breton force landed at nearby Blackpool Sands in 1404, where they were defeated on the beach by Dartmouth men.

John Hawley continued privateering to his death in 1408 and was honoured with a brass in the newly established church of St Saviour's. His son, also named John, continued his father's businesses as merchant,

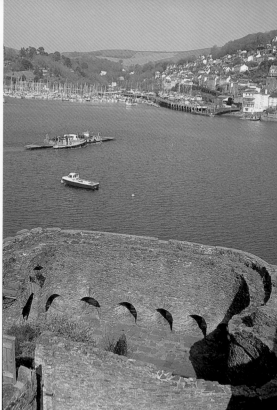

Left: The mouth of the Dart defended by Dartmouth Castle
Right: Bearscove (now Bayards Cove) Fort, the second line of defence

privateer and MP. Robert Wenyngton, who was ordered in 1449 to 'serve the king at sea' and 'clear the sea of pirates', carried on the tradition.

Advances in gun technology made Hawley's fort obsolete. The new castle (page 20), built mainly between 1481 and 1494, was the first in England with guns as its major armament. A second castle was built opposite at Kingswear, from where a chain boom could be stretched right across the river. In 1509, Henry VIII ordered Bearscove Castle on Bayard's Cove as an extra line of defence.

Thus secured, Dartmouth played a leading part defeating Philip II's Armada in 1588. It provided two ships fully armed and victualled, *Cressant* (70 men) and *Harte* (30 men). Both returned safely. Dartmouth also contributed 92 land soldiers. In addition, nine more ships carrying over 600 men were fitted out by local gentry and merchants.

The Dart nurtured several of England's greatest Elizabethan seamen and explorers. John Davis of Stoke Gabriel was the most celebrated navigator of his day. He explored the coasts of Greenland and Baffin Island, looking for the elusive North West Passage. Searching for a route to China, he sailed to the Magellan Straits and the East Indies. His charts, books and notes were of immense value to other navigators then and later. His name is remembered in Davis Strait, in the Canadian Arctic.

Sir Humphrey Gilbert of Greenway, a half brother of Sir Walter Raleigh, annexed Newfoundland for his Queen in 1583. However, Dartmouth fishermen were already prominent among those from several nations exploiting the rich Newfoundland Banks.

Fleets of Dartmouth ships sailed out each season. Newfoundland cod formed the basis of its prosperity for the next two centuries. Profits were boosted when returns from selling the dried cod ('toerag') to Mediterranean countries bought a second cargo of fruits and wine for sale, along with the remaining fish and fish oil.

Dartmouth exported Devon cloth in quantity. Trade expanded and Dartmouth merchants grew rich, building many handsome houses between 1570 and 1640 – most notably the Butterwalk (page 10) – on newly reclaimed land.

Commercially oriented with a strong Puritan element, Dartmouth largely supported Parliament in the Civil War. Both Dartmouth and Kingswear castles were manned and armed, as were the church towers and ships in the harbour, but the town surrendered to Prince Maurice, the King's nephew, in 1643 after losing 17 men in a siege. The Royalists built earthworks at Gallants Bower above the Castle and at the Redoubt, Kingswear. In 1646 they surrendered in their turn to General Fairfax.

Trade revived eventually after the upheavals of war and Dartmouth's wealth was reflected in many fine Georgian buildings; the 1737 Custom House at Bayard's Cove is a prime example. The American War of Independence interrupted Dartmouth's vital trade with Newfoundland and the American colonies, but the town fitted out 58 privateers, capturing 35 ships.

Shipbuilding orders from the Navy helped offset commercial losses in the Napoleonic Wars.

With the Continent closed to tourists, the English upper class took more holidays at home. The habit stuck and the Dart Valley enjoyed lasting popularity, especially after the royal yacht, *Victoria and Albert*, called in 1846.

'This place is lovely,' wrote Queen Victoria, 'with its wooded rocks, church and castle… It puts me much in mind of the Rhine.' She called again in 1856 and gave £25 to the Regatta, which became 'Royal' thereafter. Handsome villas sprang up on both sides of the Dart Estuary, many built for visiting yachtsmen.

When the naval training vessels *Britannia* and *Hindustan* were moored in the Dart (in 1863 and 1865 respectively), the town gained another source of income, much enhanced by the arrival of the railway in 1864.

As steam replaced sail, Dartmouth and Kingswear developed a lucrative coal bunkering trade, although shipbuilding remained the biggest employer.

Dartmouth in 1946. Notice the different approach by road. College Road was constructed only in the 1970s

An industrial and naval centre, Dartmouth was much involved in the World Wars. Between 1939 and 1945, it witnessed the greatest volume of shipping it had ever known, drawing the dangerous attentions of the Luftwaffe in 667 air raid alerts. In 1942 Philips' Shipyard was attacked and 23 people killed. A year later 14 died when central Dartmouth was bombed and the Butterwalk so badly damaged it was threatened with demolition.

Dartmouth was packed with ships and servicemen in the build-up to D-Day. Britannia Royal Naval College was filled with Americans and Coronation Park with Nissen huts. All the way up to Dittisham, ramps and hards were built along the river. The shipyards were a hive of activity. Philip & Son alone produced 230 vessels during the War.

Shipbuilding continued until the 1970s, fading out like the coal bunkering trade before it. The old yards became marinas. Pleasure craft came to dominate the river which, along with Dartmouth's superb natural setting and range of historic buildings, remains the town's greatest asset now that leisure and tourism are the chief industries.

The stages of land reclamation

Dartmouth in the early Middle Ages was two settlements, Hardness and Clifton, hemmed in by steep hillsides and separated by a tidal creek. The Quay area at the centre of modern Dartmouth was under water at high tide, as were what are now the Market, the main car park, Coronation Park and the Royal Avenue Gardens. The water reached as far west as Ford and as far north as Undercliff.

Over the centuries, this muddy creek has been reclaimed and the river progressively embanked to create more building land, to protect Dartmouth from spring tides and to enable ships to moor in deeper water.

Medieval Hardness was established on the rocky headland or 'ness' just north of the creek, at the junction of Ridge Hill and Clarence Street, where the Ship in Dock (an old inn rebuilt in 1821) now stands. Hardness provided a 'hard' where vessels could tie up. Until the 1930s, Hardness overlooked shipbuilding yards.

South of the creek, Clifton clung, as its name suggests, to the steep slopes rising out of the river. Today, the streets of Dartmouth rise tier on tier, joined by steps, in a centuries old pattern. Indeed, the streets were all too steep for wheeled vehicles and Dartmouth was served by packhorses until 1823, when Victoria Road was built to connect it to the turnpike network.

In 1243 a 'foss' (dam) was built across the creek to impound the water in the Mill Pool so that it could drive tidal mills. The dam, which gave its name to Foss Street, thus connected Clifton and Hardness, although the mill owners tried (unsuccessfully) to stop townsfolk using it as a short cut. The southern end of the Foss led to St Saviour's and the commercial heart of Clifton: Smith Street, Lower Street and Higher Street. This area retains Dartmouth's best surviving medieval buildings, including the Cherub (see page 14).

Expanding trade led to a land shortage. Dartmouth Corporation started an ambitious programme of reclamation in 1570, transforming the town over the following seventy years by building New Quay, Spithead and the Butterwalk. Happily, the Butterwalk and a fine terrace of 17th century houses along the Boat Float to Fairfax Place survive to show the wealth and vision of Dartmouth's merchants.

The New Ground (now Royal Avenue Gardens) was first reclaimed

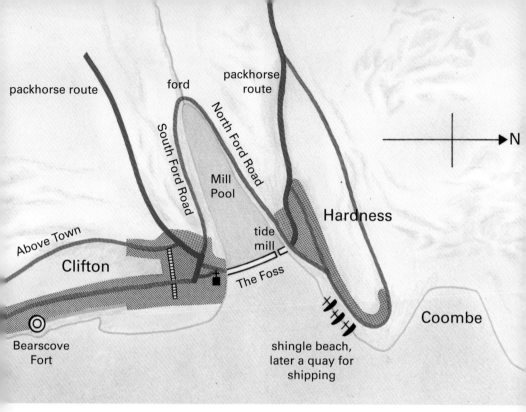

Dartmouth consisted originally of two settlements, Hardness and Clifton. They were connected by the 'foss' in 1243 and land has been reclaimed by stages ever since. Compare this with the map on page 12

in 1671, when entries for 'carrying ballast' there to build up a sand-bank first appear. Unfortunately, it proved unstable and the tide once nearly washed it away. The Butterwalk also proved unstable. The re-claimed land it was built on had to be shored up with a strong stone wall, which made an extra quay for ships to dock at.

Dartmouth's next major advance came in 1828, when the Market was built on part of the site of the old Mill Pool, which had been silt-ing up for centuries. In 1878 the Pool between Mayor's Avenue and the New Ground was filled in – it had long been used as a cesspool and was recognized as a health hazard.

Dartmouth was further enlarged with the Embankment in 1885, which was extended a further six metres in 1986. Coombe Mud became Coronation Park as late as 1937, when the North Embankment was completed to cope with increased car and tourist traffic.

The Butterwalk, distinguished by lavishly detailed carving

Exploring the town centre on foot

Central Dartmouth is compact and full of interest – ideal for exploration on foot. This tour could be completed in an hour, but there is so much to see it could easily occupy half a day. See the map on page 12.

1. Start from the Tourist Information Centre, which has helpful staff and a good range of local books and leaflets. Next door is the Newcomen Memorial Engine, honouring Dartmouth's pioneering mechanical engineer, Thomas Newcomen (see page 22).

Cross the road to the Flavel Methodist and United Reform Church, built in 1895 in remembrance of the celebrated non-conformist preacher John Flavel (1630-1691). Flavel served as Vicar of Townstal from 1656 up to his ejection under Charles II's intolerant regime in 1662. Until the 'Glorious Revolution' of 1688, he was a secret pastor, serving non-conformists in the Dartmouth area. His memorial is in the church.

Behind the church is the Flavel Centre, housing Dartmouth's new library. The Centre – a venue for local art exhibitions – and its café are open all year. The auditorium *cum* theatre and cinema hosts live music and community events.

Opposite the church are the Royal Avenue Gardens. Originally known as the New Ground, the site was reclaimed from mudflats in the 1670s to provide additional moorings for ships. For 200 years it remained an island, linked to the Quay by a bridge. In Victoria's reign it was laid out as a formal garden with the obligatory bandstand of the era. This is still much used for concerts and during Dartmouth's Music Festival each May. Close to the entrance is the first of several blue plaques on this walk – this one commemorates Corporal Theodore Veale VC.

2. Pause at the junction of the Quay and Duke Street. The weather vane on the bank building portrays a cog, the trading vessel that helped establish Dartmouth's highly profitable wine trade with Bordeaux. Duke Street contains the grandest Butterwalk in Devon, if not in England. As in the Butterwalks at Totnes and Plympton St Maurice, a series of granite piers support the upper floors of buildings projecting over the street, providing a covered market.

Dartmouth's Butterwalk consists of four splendid timber framed houses built between 1628 and 1640. After serious bomb damage during the Second World War, they were beautifully restored.

The upper floors are profusely carved, whilst the interiors are graced with wonderful plasterwork, best seen in the Sloping Deck Restaurant, where the overmantel depicts the Pentecost with Moses and David. All the figures are in 17th century costume and oblivious to the remarkable sloping floor, caused by subsidence on soft, reclaimed ground.

Dartmouth Museum at the near end of the Butterwalk also has excellent plasterwork ceilings and linenfold panelling, especially the overmantel in the King's Room. This bears the Stuart Royal Coat of Arms: Charles II is said to have been received here by the Mayor of Dartmouth in 1671 – one assumes Rev. Flavel was not invited.

Like the rest of the Butterwalk, the museum reflects the prosperity brought by Newfoundland cod and the export of Devon cloth. The pole staircase is a recycled ship's mast, as is the Cherub's, Higher Street. When the Butterwalk was built, ships moored at the rear of the buildings and discharged their cargoes directly.

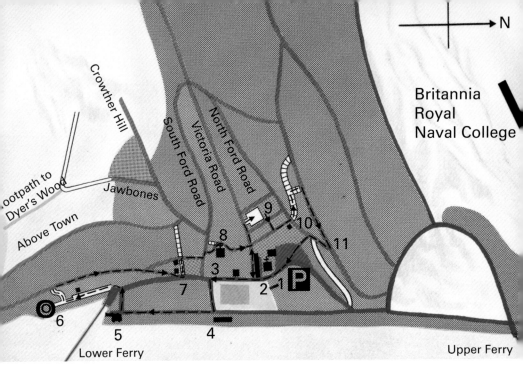

Leaving the Museum, cross Duke Street and walk along the Quay. Built between 1584 and 1640 from reclaimed mudflats, the Quay and its neighbouring streets retain Devon's best collection of 17th century merchants' houses – and some exuberant Victorian imitations, with pargeting, slate hanging and iron cresting, far outdoing the originals.

Centre stage on the Quay is the Royal Castle Hotel, much older than its handsome 1835 façade suggests. The hotel began in 1639 as two merchants' houses, though some of the roof beams – recycled ships' spars – may be older.

During the 18th century, one of the merchants' houses was known as the New Inn. By 1777, both houses were combined, with a brew house and stables at the rear. The Customs and Excise held a sale at the Castle Inn that year of 'a quantity of Bordeaux Claret and French White Wine, duty free and sufficient to raise £353 payment of salvage' – an interesting insight into Dartmouth life.

The remarkable top-lit staircase hall with its magnificent bell board was built in the old courtyard in 1835, when a third floor and the façade were all added. When a new turnpike road was built in 1823, the Castle prospered as a coaching inn and restyled itself as a hotel.

After visits by the Prince of Wales it became the Royal Castle Hotel

The Russian cannon at the far end of the Embankment

in 1902. Prince Charles and Prince Andrew have visited the hotel, and it served as a film set for Agatha Christie's *Ordeal by Innocence*. Other visitors include the seafarers Sir Francis Chichester, Chay Blyth and Alec Rose. Film stars Cary Grant, Gregory Peck, Diana Dors and Faye Dunnaway added further glamour. The Royal Castle has a wealth of historic artefacts, including swords and muskets. The 300-year-old range in the bar is still used for spit roasting.

Continue along the Quay past the Boat Float to the junction with Fairfax Place.

3. The corner building is 16th century. Turn left, towards the Station Restaurant. When the railway from Paignton to Kingswear opened in 1864 the journey to Dartmouth was completed by ferry – so the station never saw a train, though it did sell railway tickets. York House at the junction with South Embankment was built in 1893.

4. Turn right along South Embankment. The Harbour Office has a blue plaque for Samuel Lake, an engineer who planned the Embankment and promoted Dartmouth's profitable coal bunkering trade. At the far end of the Embankment is a Russian cannon, *prix de guerre* from the Crimean War.

The Cherub, which is Dartmouth's only complete medieval building. It was a house (perhaps with the ground floor used as a workplace and shop) but is now an inn. The original pole staircase and other carpentry can be clearly seen inside

5. Turn right, then left to Bayard's Cove Inn, much restored, but retaining many fascinating original features. Walk past the Dartmouth Arms onto cobbled Bayard's Cove. Lined with attractive 17th to early 19th century houses, it was used in filming BBC's *The Onedin Line* – photographs can be seen in the Dartmouth Arms. The grandest building is the Old Custom House dating from 1739. Gull Cottage bears a 1710 fire insurance mark and a plaque to another Dartmouth sailor and explorer, Sir Humphrey Gilbert (see page 6).

6. At the far end of Bayard's Cove is Bayard's Cove Fort, originally called Bearscove Castle, a small artillery fort with eleven gunports built in 1510 to protect the town. From the Castle, take the narrow alleyway up Castle Steps. At the top turn right down Newcomen Road, lined on one side with attractive Georgian houses. Keep right when the road forks. On the right here is a plaque to John Hawley, merchant, shipmaster and fourteen times Mayor of Dartmouth. Almost opposite is a plaque to Newcomen. At the foot used to be the Harbour Bookshop, founded in 1951 by Christopher Robin Milne, son of A A Milne and hero of the Christopher Robin stories – which he refused to stock.

7. Turn left and almost immediately turn left again up Horn Hill Steps to the Cherub. Built circa 1380, it is the oldest secular building in Dartmouth and its only complete medieval house. Turn first right along Higher Street which has more medieval houses on the right (undergoing restoration after fire damage at the time of writing). These were originally the shambles (butchers' shops) at the medieval heart of Dartmouth. The stocks and pillory provided further amusement. Turn left and immediately right past the Seven Stars to St Saviour's. Built in 1372, the church has many interesting features (see page 17).

8. Turn right out of the church into St Saviour's Square. Town Cottage was once part of Dartmouth Gaol. Turn left up Collaford Steps. At the top is a notice banning wheelbarrows and hand carts. Walk back down the steps and follow Anzac Street to Duke Street. Turn left along Victoria Road and right through a gateway to enter the Old Market. Built as a pannier market on reclaimed land in 1828, this has been recently refurbished.

9. On the far side of the Old Market is Market Square, full of stalls on market days. Leave the square to the right of the Dolphin Inn, along Union Street. Turn left into Foss Street, which has a range of galleries and shops housed in 17th and 18th century buildings.

10. At the far end, cross the street ahead, opposite Broadstone House, and take the steps up Brown's Hill. This was the packhorse route to Townstal. Before Victoria Road was built in 1823, there was no route for wheeled traffic into Dartmouth. Opposite 'Grey Stones', turn right up another flight of steps, then right onto Clarence Hill. Named in honour of the Duke of Clarence (later William IV), who visited in 1828, this medieval street is lined with handsome houses.

11. At the bottom of Clarence Hill, turn sharp right into Broadstone. Walk past the Old Bakehouse to the George and Dragon. On the left is Undercliff, the original shoreline. Continue along Broadstone and turn first left at Zion Place into Mayor's Avenue. The Tourist Information Centre is straight ahead.

The masterly ironwork on the medieval door of St Saviour's depicts the Tree of Life with the lions of Edward I. Although dated 1631 (when the church was substantially repaired), its design is thoroughly medieval

St Saviour's

It was a long trek uphill from the new town of Dartmouth to the church of St Clement at Townstal; hence St Saviour's was begun around 1330, despite opposition from the Bishop of Exeter. Consecrated in 1372, it wins a place in Simon Jenkins's *England's Thousand Best Churches*, especially for its superb medieval door. The beautifully carved and painted Rood screen (1496) is characteristically Devon, its patterns of ropes entwined with grapes recalling the Bordeaux wine trade. Hidden among the foliage is a green man, a pagan figure associated with spring, whilst saints occupy the lower panels, some carrying the instruments of their martyrdom. Also late 15th century is the wineglass pulpit; of impressive size and richly painted, it is carved in stone.

Dartmouth's leading man, John Hawley, was also the major benefactor of St Saviour's. His chancel brass dates from 1408 (look for it under the carpet) and shows him in full armour with his two wives. Also of note is the font, probably as old as the oldest part of the church, and the Arms of Charles II, recalling his visit in 1673.

The High Altar is curious: although Victorian, it incorporates the four carved Evangelists of 1588. They were the legs of the communion table which replaced the stone altar at the Reformation.

Opposite: Dartmouth's Boat Float is surrounded by an attractive medley of historic buildings, notably the Royal Castle Hotel (see pages 12-13)

A wide variety of vessels may be seen on the Dart, especially during the annual August Royal Regatta and Air show

A walk from the Quay to the Castle via Dyer's Hill

This 2 km (1¼ mile) walk entails a steep climb to Dyer's Hill – rewarded by magnificent views. Allow plenty of time as there is a great deal of interest to see, especially St Saviour's church (page 17) and the Castle and St Petrox (pages 20-21). A longer (7 km) version of the walk can be found in *Shortish Walks – Torbay and Dartmouth*.

Turn left out of the Tourist Information Centre and right up Duke Street, past the Butterwalk. Turn left into Anzac Street to St Saviour's. Climb the steps in the far right corner of the square and turn right into South Ford Road.

(To your left is medieval Smith Street, possibly named after Geoffrey the Goldsmith who lived here in 1310, rubbing shoulders with many fellow tradesmen and shopkeepers. The name South Ford Road gives a clue to Dartmouth's early development. It led along the creekside to a ford linking the two early medieval hamlets which later grew into a bustling port as trade increased and the mudflats were drained.)

Turn almost immediately left at the old water conduit (one of a series supplying Dartmouth) and climb Crowther's Hill, an old packhorse track. Fork right and continue steeply up Crowther's Hill. Take the next turning left, Jawbones. Past the new houses, the road narrows to its original width, a track.

When this track bends sharply, cross the stile ahead into a field for a stunning view of the whole Dart Estuary. The protection offered by the twin castles of Dartmouth and Kingswear can be readily appreciated. Likewise, you can see the excellent shelter given by the sinuous curves of the Dart and how the former mudflats have been built up to form Dartmouth's Quay and neighbouring streets. Presiding grandly over the whole scene is Britannia Royal Naval College (see page 23).

Follow the path ahead through the field. Walk in front of a wooden bench. Keep to the same path and ignore side paths made by animals. Continue into the wood. When the path divides, turn left and downhill via a series of hairpin bends. On the way down, you will cross two level terraces – former rope walks, where ship's rope was twisted and stretched. Steps lead down to Above Town.

Turn right and follow Above Town, which descends steeply. Turn right into Warfleet Road. Take the next left, Castle Road, signed for Dartmouth Castle. This circuits around Warfleet Creek via two pairs of disused limekilns – a path on the far side of the creek leads to the foot of one.

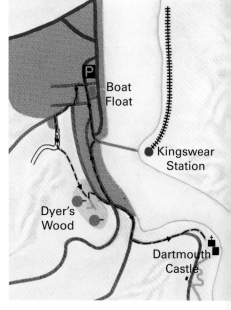

The road forks. Keep left, following the signed Coast Path parallel to the road. When it rejoins the road, cross over and continue along the Coast Path to St Petrox, the Castle and Castle Cove.

Either retrace your steps to the start (but perhaps not climbing Dyer's Hill) or take the ferry from the small jetty just below the Coast Path.

The Castle and St Petrox

Defending the Dart was vital to Dartmouth's shipping, indeed to England's safety. In 1387 the French assembled a massive invasion force. John Hawley was acutely aware of the danger. As mayor, he appealed to Richard II, who authorized him to build a 'fortalice'. Of this first castle, one tower, part of a curtain wall and a dry moat remain behind the present castle.

Dartmouth Castle has since been developed over the centuries to meet changing threats and newer weapons. Most of the castle as seen today is late 15th century, when advances in gun technology had rendered Hawley's 'fortalice' obsolete. The innovative three storey Gun Tower (1481) was the first in England to have guns as its major armament; they were placed as close to the waterline as possible to inflict maximum damage. This proved a highly effective deterrent when combined with the chain boom stretched across the river's mouth from Dartmouth's twin castle on the Kingswear shore.

Henry VIII's break with Rome in 1539 increased international tension and a massive coastal defence programme from Kent to Cornwall was launched: Dartmouth Castle's defences were further strengthened with two more gun platforms north and south of the Gun Tower. A further gun battery was added in 1544.

Victorian guns, along with reproduction Tudor and Medieval weapons, are fired during historical re-enactments

All this time, Dartmouth Castle encompassed a chapel, which had stood before the Castle was ever built. In the 1630s, this was rebuilt as St Petrox church. It has several interesting features, including a 1641 pulpit, a Norman font and a 1609 brass.

Designed to protect Dartmouth from naval attack, Dartmouth Castle was vulnerable from the landward side, especially from long range guns mounted on the nearby hilltops, as proved when Royalist soldiers backed by artillery took it in 1643. The Royalists then set about fortifying the most threatening hilltops – Gallants Bower above Dartmouth Castle and Mount Ridley overlooking Kingswear. However, when the Parliamentarians retook Dartmouth in 1646 the two new fortifications surrendered the next day and Dartmouth Castle the day after.

In the late 1850s revolutionary new 'ironclads', led by France's *La Gloire*, posed a new threat. The Castle's seaward battery was completely rebuilt and rearmed in 1861 and again in 1889.

The Castle was pressed into service once more during the Second World War, when two 4.7 inch naval guns were installed. A new battery was built on the Kingswear shore with two 6 inch guns and searchlight units, whilst an anti-submarine net (reminiscent of the 15th century chain boom) was stretched across the river. Dartmouth Castle is now open to the public through English Heritage (01803 833588).

The Museum and the Newcomen engine

The Newcomen Memorial Engine at the Tourist Information Centre shows the remarkable invention of Thomas Newcomen (1663-1729) in motion. An unassuming Dartmouth ironmonger and zealous Baptist, Newcomen was one of the world's great inventors. His 1712 reciprocating steam engine, working at atmospheric pressure, was a great technical advance and the model for all later engines. It contributed immensely to industrial development. For sixty years it dominated mining, raising as much water from deep mines in two days as fifty men and 20 horses could in a week.

William Henley was also a Dartmouth ironmonger and self-taught scientist, naturalist and artist. His wonderful Victorian collections, including his drawings of Dartmouth, his slides and specimens, are to be found in the excellent Museum on the Butterwalk, which includes interactive displays and children's activities.

One of the oldest and finest buildings in town, the Museum has extensive and varied collections. As well as a splendid photographic archive, there is a 30 minute archive film of Dartmouth preparing for D-Day (see page 7). The King's Room has a beautiful ceiling and carved wooden panelling. It tells the story of maritime Dartmouth with cleverly crafted model ships, both sail and steam. Of special interest is the *Mayflower*, in which the Pilgrim Fathers sailed and which called at Dartmouth on its way to America. A second room shows the social history of the town.

Naval cadet training at Dartmouth

Naval cadet training began at Dartmouth in 1863, when the wooden hulk HMS *Britannia* was moored in the Dart. She was joined in 1865 by HMS *Hindustan*. Dartmouth's prestige was raised in 1877 when Princes Albert Victor and George (later George V) were trained here. However, cadet numbers increased and serious questions were raised about their health on the overcrowded hulks – a form of accommodation previously used for prisoners.

A specialised shore-based training college was called for and Dartmouth was chosen, despite fierce competition from Portsmouth. Work on Britannia Royal Naval College (BRNC) began in 1898 and was completed in 1905.

The Britannia Royal Naval College

Its grand and imposing style, aided by its splendid hillside setting, is characteristic of its era and architect. Aston (later Sir Aston) Webb designed many important public buildings such as Admiralty Arch and frontages of Buckingham Palace and the Victoria and Albert Museum.

Hindustan was towed to Plymouth in 1905 and used as an artificers' training ship. In 1914 a new accommodation block was begun at BRNC and *Britannia* was towed off to the scrap yard in 1916 to the strains of 'Rule Britannia'.

With Dartmouth a prime target in the Second World War, and a supply of naval officers vital for the war effort, the cadets were evacuated to safety at Eaton Hall, Cheshire and 700 WRNS installed at the college. One died during a subsequent air raid. In November 1943 the WRNS made way for American officers preparing for D-Day.

After the war the status quo was resumed. Prince Charles and Prince Andrew followed the Duke of Edinburgh in training at BRNC. After the Royal Naval College, Greenwich, closed in 1998, it remained the only establishment through which all new naval officers must pass.

Guided tours of BRNC are available through Dartmouth TIC.

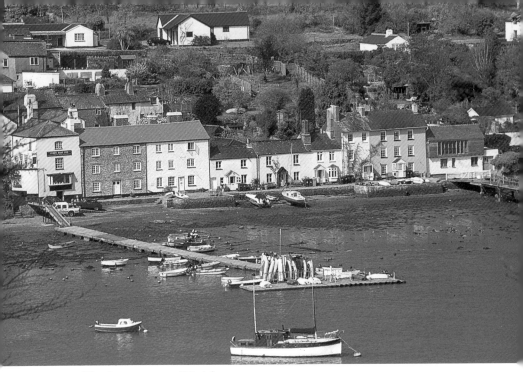

The ferry quay at Dittisham

Dittisham

Dittisham is one of Devon's most attractive riverside villages. The boat trip there from Dartmouth is a real pleasure – as is the Dart Valley Trail for energetic walkers. Salmon fishing and river-borne trade were village mainstays in the past, but sailing is predominant today. Visitors can hire a boat or join a river cruise to Bow Creek, Stoke Gabriel or Sharpham Vineyard.

Dittisham's streets are a medley of vernacular buildings in stone and slate, cob and thatch, including a beautiful church and two historic inns. The Ferry Boat Inn is thought to be 17th century and features a large fireplace with blazing log fire and exposed ceiling beams. The wonderful views across 'Dittisham Lake' are a special feature. BRNC cadets – Princes Charles and Andrew among them – have left an intriguing collection of RN insignia.

Walk up the main street. The Red Lion dates from around 1750 and retains two open fires and a pleasant beer garden. Among the fascinating period photographs is one of the Dittisham Ferry with the postmistress and a donkey and another of salmon netting.

The Dart, seen from the gardens of Greenway House (National Trust)

St George's is late medieval. The red sandstone font is Norman; the wineglass pulpit of carved stone and the screen are 15th century, whilst the aisle windows by Pugin are Victorian.

Ferries and boat trips: www.greenwayferry.co.uk (01803) 882811

Greenway House and Gardens

No one visiting Dittisham should miss Greenway House and Gardens (National Trust, 01803 842382). Ring the brass bell by the Ferry Boat Inn to summon the ferry, follow the lane uphill and then the signed path through the gardens.

Alternatively, drive there via Kingswear and Galmpton (seven miles) but drivers need to book parking in advance on 01803 842382.

As well as superb views of the river, Greenway Gardens offers thirteen hectares (thirty acres) of wildflowers and native trees, camellias, rhododendrons and exotics from all over the world.

Greenway House was the holiday home of crime writer Agatha Christie and her second husband, archaeologist Max Mallowan. It is packed with their various antique collections and memorabilia, most interestingly from archaeological trips.

Kingswear and Coleton Fishacre

The best views of Kingswear, with its attractive Victorian villas rising in tiers, are from Dartmouth Quay and from our walk to the Castle (pages 18-19), whilst some of the best of views of Dartmouth are from Kingswear.

Kingswear is linked to Dartmouth by two ferries. The Higher Ferry or 'floating bridge' was originally driven by steam and built at the same time as the new Brixham road in 1832.

Kingswear's most interesting buildings stand by the Lower Ferry which was first recorded in 1365 but may well be older than that.

The Royal Dart began as the Plume of Feathers, but changed its name to the Station Hotel when the railway from Paignton arrived in 1864. It retains the Italianate station clock with 'GWR' (Great Western Railway). As the Dart Yacht Club met here, it was renamed the Yacht Hotel. When Queen Victoria patronized Dartmouth Regatta, it became the Royal Dart Hotel.

During the Second World War the Royal Navy requisitioned it to control several Motor Gun Boat, Motor Torpedo Boat and Motor Launch Flotillas. Co-operating with French Resistance, they smuggled

Coleton Fishacre, once the home of the D'Oyly Carte family

secret agents into occupied France and smuggled Allied aviators back. Sub-Lieutenant de Gaulle (son of General Charles de Gaulle) and Lieutenant François Mitterrand – later President of France – were among the French servicemen stationed here.

The railway gave Kingswear, an active trading port until around 1700, a new commercial life. Coal wagons for the bunkering trade and Dartmouth's gas works lined the sidings and passenger coaches brought increasing numbers of visitors. Happily, the line was saved by the Dart Valley Railway Company in 1972. It also saved the stations through to Paignton, including Kingswear's – you may recognize it from the film *The French Lieutenant's Woman*.

A four mile drive or a three mile hike over the beautiful but steep coast path will take you to Coleton Fishacre (National Trust, 01803 752466), built of local stone for the D'Oyly Carte family in 1925.

It has much operatic memorabilia, especially of Gilbert and Sullivan productions, and reflects the best of the Arts and Crafts movement in design and furnishings. A wind dial and a three dimensional map of the coast are special features, whilst the gardens offer year-round colour from a variety of rare and exotic plants.

The Round Robin Trip

Allow a full day for the Round Robin to Totnes and Paignton. A wonderful combination of boat, bus (usually open top) and steam train, it is packed with historical interest and offers a rich variety of scenery: river, rolling hills and coast. Take binoculars and a camera.

You can begin at any of the main points and do the trip either way round, but please be sure to co-ordinate the tidal river cruise with the steam trains. A little planning allows you to explore Totnes with its medieval streets, castle and museums.

Board the boat at Dartmouth pontoon. You will pass Britannia Royal Naval College, Greenway and Dittisham, followed by Dittisham Lake, Stoke Gabriel and Sharpham vineyard. The densely wooded river served as the Amazon in the BBC's *Onedin Line*. You are unlikely to meet naked tribesmen, though canoes are a possibility, as are heron, cormorant and seals.

Disembark at Totnes. Board the Paignton bus here. Alternatively, explore the town by following the quay upriver. Turn left and left again across Totnes Bridge (1828), still the lowest bridging point on the Dart. A stone bridge probably replaced an older timber one in the 13th century. Before that there was a ford.

Totnes had a 10th century mint and was an established port by the late 11th, with its own coastal fleet. Using the existing Saxon fortified settlement, the Normans raised the superb castle keep which stands

Kingswear Station, with a train departing for Paignton

in front of you, overlooking the town. The castle was enlarged and rebuilt in 1336 (English Heritage, 01803 864406).

The cloth trade made Totnes and its seaport, Dartmouth, rich. Walk up Fore Street, where wealthy merchants have left us one of the most interesting Elizabethan streets in England. Totnes Museum at number 70 is splendid, with its carved, overhanging jetties; the Butterwalk presents a fine medley of 16th and 17th century houses.

The cloth trade declined and so did river traffic. Totnes continued as a market town. However, like Dartmouth, it played an important role in the Second World War. Corvettes and minesweepers built in Totnes were floated downriver. Fitted with engines at Dartmouth, they were hidden in the estuary until needed.

Enjoy the bus journey to Paignton, with its vista of rolling hills reaching to Dartmoor. Then the beautiful seven mile rail journey to Kingswear includes sea and river views. For the engineers its hills and cliffs presented many problems, solved by three large viaducts and a 400 metre long tunnel. Alight at Kingswear station by the Royal Dart (page 26). Board the Lower Ferry for Dartmouth.

For booking and information: www.dartmouthrailriver.co.uk (01803 555872).

Opposite: South Hallsands was once a thriving fishing village. Built on a raised beach, it was largely destroyed by the sea following offshore dredging, as the information boards explain

Left: The lighthouse at Start Point. It is 28m (87ft) tall and has seasonal opening – 01803 771802 www.trinityhouse.co.uk

There are marvellous walks along the coast path in either direction from Start Point

A drive to Slapton, Hallsands and Start Point

Distance: 30 miles/49km   Time: Nearly two hours driving, because the roads are narrow. At the height of the season, they may be very congested. There is much to see: this could well be a day trip. Map on page 32.

Start from the Park and Ride on A3122. Drive half a mile towards TOWN CENTRE. Turn right at the roundabout onto A379, STOKE FLEMING AND STRETE. Drive on for 2 miles to Stoke Fleming.

Divert right at Stoke Fleming Post Office to pass the Green Dragon. First recorded as an inn in 1607, it has period photographs and sailing memorabilia. Opposite is the ancient church, with a 13th century effigy and a 14th century brass. Drive up the lane just to the right of the church gate. At the main road, turn right, past Blackpool Sands, where Breton invaders were defeated by Dartmouth men in 1404.

Drive on through Strete. A remarkable view of Start Bay opens up. Continue downhill and take the first turning right for SLAPTON. Drive

on for 800 yards and park by the bottle bank. (Parking in Slapton itself is scarce.) Walk ahead into the village and turn right to visit the Queens Arms, the church, the Tower Inn and the Chantry Tower (1372). Retrace your steps and drive back to the main road.

Drive on for 1¹/₂ miles along the shingle ridge which separates Slapton Sands and Slapton Ley, Devon's largest freshwater lake, noted for wildfowl. Use the car park on the right at Torcross, distinguished by a Sherman tank, memorial to the 946 men who died in April 1944, when German E boats attacked during training for D-Day. Opposite the car park is the thatched Start Bay Inn. Walk 100 m down the road, to the corner of the lake, where birds often congregate.

Drive on 2 miles to Stokenham, which has two historic inns and an interesting church. Turn left at the roundabout (Carehouse Cross) for BEESANDS, PRAWLE, EAST PORTLEMOUTH. At the next junction (Mattiscombe Cross), follow the lane as it curves right, and continue following signs for START POINT.

There is a viewing table at Start Point car park and a magnificent view of Start Bay. Walk down the track for 1.1 km (²/₃ mile) to see the lighthouse. Return the way you came for 1 mile.

At Hollowcombe Head Cross turn right, SOUTH HALLSANDS. Leave your car at the car park and walk down to the Coast Path and viewing platform. Return to Dartmouth the way you came.

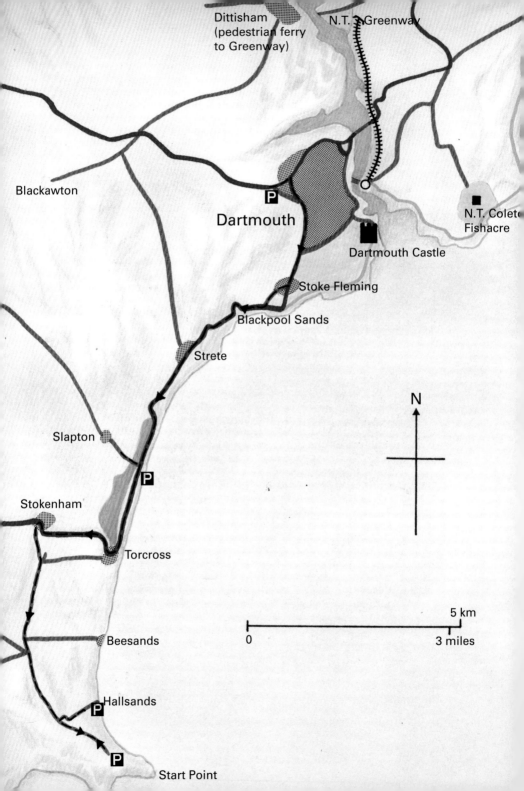